Hacking

Computer Hacking for beginners, how to hack, and understanding computer security!

Table of Contents

Introduction

Thank you for taking the time to pick up this book about hacking!

This book covers the topic of Computer hacking, what it is, and how you can learn to hack.

You will learn about the difference between white hat and black hat hacking, and be given some information on how to secure yourself against hackers.

You will learn about the different types of hackers, the hacks they do and their motivations. This book will teach you the lexicon that hackers use, and by the end of it you will be well prepared to dive into the hacking community!

At the completion of this book you will have a good understanding of how hacking and security works, and should have the ability to perform some simple hacks yourself!

Once again, thanks for reading this book, I hope that it can serve as a great introduction to your future in the hacking world!

Chapter 1:
What is Hacking?

Hacking is simply when someone exploits any weaknesses in a computer or computer network to gain entry. In regards to computer networking, hacking is a technical effort to alter the normal behavior of network connections and connected systems. Not all hacking is done with illegal or immoral intentions, and there are many classifications of hackers. The media tends to focus on the illegal form of hacking, which has given both it and the title "hacker" a negative connotation.

With the invent of bulletin-board systems, or BBS, in the 1980s, it became possible for people to upload and download information to computer networks. This is when the idea of hacking became well-known. The use of BBS peaked in 1996, when it was eclipsed by the Internet that everyone knows and uses today.

In pop-culture, one of the first references to hacking can be found in the 1982 movie *Tron*, when the main character says he has "been doing a little hacking here" while talking about breaking into a computer network. Public awareness of the idea of hacking really took off in 1983 with the release of the movie *War Games*. The idea that a group of teenagers could impact national security was frightening to many people.

As a result of the public's fear, Congressman Dan Glickman called for laws against computer hacking. In 1983, six bills were introduced to the House of Representatives on the subject. As a result of this, hackers with good intentions started to try to define and separate themselves from those with malicious ones. This is where the terms "white hat" and "black hat" hacking comes from.

In the 1990s, the term "hacker" did not have such negative connotations. Hackers were simply skilled people in computer programming and sometimes hacked a competitor to learn their code. Some hackers became good "crackers," people who were good at getting into password protected computers, networks, and files. In order to be a good cracker one had to be a good hacker. The terms became intertwined and eventually hacker won out.

Common tools of the hacker are viruses, worms, and exploits. Most people are familiar with computer viruses. It is machine code that is designed to get into a computer and start copying itself into other files and programs. A hacker can design a virus to do a number of things, resulting in minor inconveniences, all the way to devastating computer shut-downs. Viruses are able to happen due to "exploits" in a system. An exploit capitalizes on a vulnerability, bug, or glitch. An exploit will cause unexpected behavior in an operating system and applications while spreading itself. Exploits go through system networking holes and generally are used to gain more privileges than the system administrator allows. Worms are like viruses but they transport themselves over network connections.

Beginning Skills Needed to be a Successful Hacker

- Basic Computer Skills – Obviously, you have got to be good with computers. This involves more than just surfing the internet and creating Word documents. You should also know how to use the command line in Windows, edit the registry, and set-up networking parameters.

- Networking Skills – An understanding of networking is vital. Some examples of things you will need to be familiar with are:

  - DHCP

  - NAT

  - Public vs. Private IP

  - Routers and Switches

  - MAC Addressing

  - ARP

  - Subnetting

  - VLANs

  - DNS

- Linux Skills – Most tools developed for hacking use the Linux operating system. Linux gives hackers options that they cannot get using Windows. There are many online tutorials to get you started using Linux.

- Virtualization – There are several virtualization software packages, and a hacker needs to be proficient in at least one of them. Examples include VMWare Workstation and VirtualBox. This will allow you to have a safe environment to practice your hacks before using them in the real world.

- Analyzing TCP/IP Traffic and Attacks – Wireshark is a popular tool used for sniffer/protocol analysis.

Tcpdump is a command line sniffer/protocol analyzer. This will help analyze TCP/IP traffic and attacks.

- Security Technology – A good hacker has to know what they are up against. Learning how security software aims to keep out hackers is a good way to get around it. You will need to understand things like SSL (secure sockets layer,) PKI (public key infrastructure,) IDS (intrusion detection system,) and firewalls. If a beginner is serious about hacking they can learn many of these skills in a security course such as Security+.

- Wireless Technology – You will need a basic understanding of things like encryption algorithms (WEP, WPA, WPA2.) An understanding of the legal constraints on wireless technology and the protocol for authentication and connection is also useful.

- Programming – This is an utterly essential skill for even the most basic hacking. There are five programming languages that you should learn if you really want to master hacking:

  o Python – This is a high-level programming language that can be difficult for a beginner to learn. It is a scripting language, meaning you can produce a lot of code in a short period of time. There are many free online tutorials to help you learn Python. It is the choice of companies like Yahoo, Google, and NASA.

  o C - C has influenced almost all of the other programming languages, so learning it can help you pick up the others. C has a reputation for requiring complex code to perform simple tasks, making it less popular among experienced hackers. Knowledge of C still is useful when learning programming.

- o C++ - This one was originally designed to program system software, but has been used to also develop video games, and desktop, computer, and mobile apps. C++ is very fast and powerful, making it a language used by companies such as Facebook, Amazon, PayPal, and Adobe. It is considered one of the harder first languages to master.

- o Java – This language is designed to be portable, meaning it will run on any operating system, platform, or device. It is the standard programming language for mobile apps, interactive websites, and video games, making it essential to learn. Java should not be confused with JavaScript, as the first is a programming language and the second is a scripting language.

- o Ruby – This is a great first language for programmers. It is designed to read more like English. It was also designed to be fun as well as productive. Ruby gained popularity through the Ruby on Rails framework, a full-stack web framework intended for programmers to enjoy. Used most often for backend development, Ruby on Rails has been used on Shopify, Bloomberg, Airbnb, and Hulu websites.

There are varying opinions on which language should be mastered first. To learn these languages, use the internet to find free online tutorials until you begin to understand the basics and then try applying them. Most of the top hackers working today are self-taught when it comes to programming.

After mastering these beginning skills, mastering things such as web applications, forensics, database skills, scripting, reverse engineering, cryptography, and advanced TCP/IP should come next.

In order to be successful as a hacker, you must have patience, problem-solving skills, and the ability to think creatively on your feet. Persistence goes a long way, too.

Chapter 2:
Classifications of Hackers

Not all hackers set out to do the same thing and they fall at different places on the legality and morality scales. Let's talk about the different types of hackers that are out there today.

- **White-Hat Hackers** – These are essentially the good guys. They are also known as ethical hackers. White-Hat Hackers generally have a college degree in computer science or IT security and must be certified in order to have a legitimate career in hacking. The CEH (Certified Ethical Hacker) certification from the EC-Council is a popular option for people pursuing careers as ethical hackers. These hackers will help you remove a virus, provide a "PenTest" (short for penetration test) to see any weaknesses you have in your security system, and perform vulnerability assessments. They work directly for a client or for a company that makes security software.

- **Black-Hat Hackers**: Essentially, these guys are the opposite of White-Hat Hackers. They are the ones you see most in the media; the guys hacking into a banking system to steal money or putting a virus in someone's computer network. Black-Hat Hackers are also known as crackers. Identity thieves are often also Black-Hat Hackers who are using surprisingly simple tactics to steal personal information. Many hackers with nasty intent do not go after individuals but after databases instead, which is why you so often read about 100,000 plus accounts being compromised.

- **Grey-Hat Hackers:** Very little in this world is black or white, and Grey-Hat Hackers are actually the biggest group out there. These people do not steal money or information, but they also do not hack in order to help others. While they do not necessarily perform their hacks for personal gain, their activities could still be considered illegal as well as unethical.

- **Script Kiddies:** These people are unskilled hackers with very little interest in learning more about hacking. They use automated tools developed by others (usually Black-Hat Hackers) to break into computer networks. The goal of Script Kiddie is often to increase their reputation or to simply get a thrill. They usually either do not know or do not care about the implications of their hacking. Script is used to show they attack using prearranged plans and Kiddie is used to show their lack of maturity in the world of hacking. The very famous group *Anonymous* uses many tactics associated with Script Kiddies.

- **Neophytes:** Also known as a newbie or a green hat, these are hackers in training. They do not yet have many skills but unlike Script Kiddies they are trying to learn them.

- **Elite Hackers:** 2Simply a social status amongst hackers, an elite hacker is someone who has mastered many techniques and is consistently coming up with their own new ones. There are elite groups, such as *Masters of Deception*, whose members are regarded with a certain respect in the hacking community.

- **Red Hat Hackers:** Basically, these are hackers with no patience for illegal hacking. They are known as the vigilantes of the hacking world. Like White Hat Hackers, they aim to stop Black Hat Hackers but they do it by turning the tables on them. Red Hat Hackers access the attempted hacker's computer and upload viruses or use other techniques to shut down their computer.

- **Blue Hat Hackers:** These are people hired outside of a company to identify security risks so that they can be closed. This term in usually used in relation to Microsoft.

- **Hacktivists:** The intention of a Hacktivist is to use their hacking to publicize social, political, ideological, or religious messages. They generally fall into two types:

  o **Freedom of Information:** These are hacktivists that believe more, if not all, information should be available to the public and go out of their way to publish it.

  o **Cyberterrorism:** Often using website defacement and denial-or-service attacks, these hackers aim to disrupt the online lives of people and organizations they do not agree with.

- **Nation State Hackers:** These are hackers that are sanctioned by their government. Attacks done by them are considered acts of cyberwarfare. The majority of Nation State Hackers are looking for information on the U.S. Government, which is a traditional goal of espionage done in a new way. The power that Nation State Hackers have is due to the amount of resources their backing government is willing to put into them.

Chapter 3:
Types of Hacking

Hacking is a broad term used to sum up many different activities.

Black Hat Hacking

It is important to note that all of these techniques are also done by White Hat Hackers with the intention of learning the loopholes so that they can then close them.

Fake Wireless Access Points

This is one of the easiest and most common hacks. People log onto wireless networks out in public all of the time. Hackers set up fake WAPs and name them something convincing and have dozens of people connecting to their own network in minutes. At this point, any unprotected data being sent from their computer to their intended remote host can be discovered. An extra malicious twist to this is when hackers ask users to create a log-in and password to use the WAP. They can then use these to try to log-in to other sites such as Amazon, Twitter, and Facebook.

Cookie Theft

Browser cookies have an innocent enough purpose, but they are often exploited in order for a hacker to gain personal information. Cookies remember what a user does on a particular website, making their experience run smoother on that and future visits. When a hacker steals your cookies, they can use them to bypass logging on to a website and use it as if they were you. Cookie theft has been around as long as people have been using the internet. It is an ongoing battle between

White Hat and Black Hat Hackers, with White Hatters trying to make your data safe and Black Hatters developing new tools to get around security measures put in by White Hatters.

Clickjacking Attack

This attack results in the user thinking they are clicking on one thing on a website when in reality they are clicking on an opaque layer that has been hidden in the website by a hacker. In that sense, the hacker is "hijacking" clicks that are meant for one website and taking them themselves. For example, a hijacker could make you think you are typing in your password for your bank account into the bank's website, but in reality you are typing into an invisible frame being controlled by the hacker. Clickjacking is also known as a UI Redress Attack.

DoS Attack

DoS stands for Denial of Service. Unlike most attacks, a DoS attack is not an attempt to gather sensitive information (usually.) In some cases, they are used as a smokescreen to distract the website's owner while other nefarious activities are launched against them. Basically, a DoS attack is an attempt to make websites and servers unavailable to legitimate users. These attacks can last days, weeks, or even months. This length of time can result in a loss of revenue as well as consumer trust, causing potentially permanent damage to a company's reputation. Due to them being highly visible attacks, they are popular among hacktivists, extortionists, and cyber vandals.

DDoS Attack

DDoS stands for Distributed Denial of Services. The main difference between them and a DoS attack is that they DDoS attack comes from many computers while a DoS originates from just one. DDoS attacks often utilize botnets. In this attack, a machine or a server is made unavailable to its users. The hacker then takes advantage of the system being offline to alter the website to their own liking. Generally, the goal is to temporarily take down a website so that a goal can be achieved or to permanently take down a once successfully running system. The most common way or orchestrating this attack is to flood the system with URL requests in a very short amount of time. This "bottlenecking" of the system will cause the server's CPU to run out of resources.

File Name Tricks

This trick involves naming a file something that would entice a user to click on it, like amazingcoupons.exe.zip. When the user clicks, the malware would be downloaded on the computer, not amazing coupons. More sophisticated hackers can use Unicode character to affect the output of the name of the file presented to users.

SQL Injecting

A code injection technique, it is commonly used to attack data-driven applications. Immoral SQL statements are implanted into an entry field for execution. A common goal is to dump the database's contents into the attacker's possession. SQL attacks allow the hacker to basically control a website, deleting information, negating transactions, changing balances, and making the information public knowledge. In order for a SQL injection to be successful, there must be a security vulnerability to exploit.

Phishing

This is an attempt to gain information by masquerading as a legitimate company with a legitimate reason to be asking for it. The goal is usually to obtain usernames, passwords, and credit card details. Phishing is a major threat to people's online security, especially with the popularity of social media sites. There are several types of phishing, including:

- Email/Spam: The most common type of phishing, hackers send out millions of emails hoping for a few people to fall for it. These emails usually ask people to act urgently to verify their account or their identity by putting in their credentials.

- Web Based Delivery: A more sophisticated type of phishing, this is also known as "man-in-the-middle" phishing. The hacker creates a point in between the user and the legitimate website and phishes for information during legitimate transactions. The user often has no idea anything unusual happened.

- Instant Messaging: The hacker sends the user an instant message that contains a link that looks like it leads to a legitimate website. The user will be asked to put personal information into the fake phishing website.

- Search Engines: This method involves search engine ads that look legit but when the user tries to make a purchase or apply for the credit card being advertised their information is stolen.

- Malware: Done through emails, the user must click on a link or download something that, unbeknownst to them, allows the malware to run on their computer.

Pharming

Similar to phishing, pharming directs users to bogus websites in order to gain information such as usernames, passwords, and account information. The bogus website is designed to look like a legitimate one. When a user enters a website in their browser, it is translated into an IP address via a DNS server. The computer then stores the DNS information so it does not have to access the server every time. If a pharmer successfully poisons a user's DNS cache they can have a common web address lead to a fake site of their choosing.

Keystroke Logging

Often used in conjunction with phishing, it is keeping track of what keys are being pressed and what touch-points are being used. It is used to figure out and record passwords and usernames. The most common way to get one on a device is through a Trojan delivered by a phishing email.

Packet Sniffing

This is a tool used by hackers for monitoring activities on your network. Unencrypted passwords, credit card information, and other sensitive data can be stolen this way. In many of the cases of mass credit card theft, a packet sniffer was used and the victim of the breach was not using encrypted data. If a hacker manages to get their hands on an unencrypted administrator password, they have the power to do whatever they want on a network.

White Hat Hacking

White Hat Hackers use the same techniques as Black Hat Hackers while testing the security of a website or server. The biggest service a White Hat Hacker provides is running a PenTest.

Penetration Test

Companies or individuals hire ethical hackers to run penetration tests, or PenTests, on their servers. These tests can be performed manually but are often automated. There are several security-assessment tools available to help run the test.

- Specialized Operating Systems Distributions: These usually contain a set of pre-packaged and pre-configured tools to help run the PenTest. There are several available:

    o Kali Linux, which is based on Debian Linux

    o Pentoo, which is based on Gentoo Linux

    o WHAX, which is based on Slackware Linux

- Software Framework: This is software that provides a generic function that can be altered by the user to suit their specific purpose. For PenTests, there are several popular choices:

    o Nmap (Network Mapper)

    o Metasploit Project

    o w3af (Web Application Attack and Audit Framework)

o   Burp Suite

o   OWASP Zap

Ultimately, when an ethical hacker performs a PenTest, they start with reconnaissance (where they gather information about the target,) then identify possible entry points, attempt to break in, and then report back their findings.

Chapter 4:
Computer Viruses

No computer user ever wants to hear that they have been infected with a virus. The most expensive computer virus in history was called MyDoom and cost an estimated 38.5 billion dollars. This number is particularly staggering if you consider that 68% of money lost as a result of cyber-attacks is considered unrecoverable. A computer virus is a software program designed to intentionally enter a computer without the user's permission. It has the ability to replicate and spread. It is true that some viruses do little other than replicate, but you should never knowingly leave a virus on your computer thinking it is harmless.

Let's talk about how malicious hackers, more accurately known as crackers, use viruses and how you can protect yourself from some of the more popular types.

Direct Action Virus

The goal of this virus is to replicate itself and to take action when it is executed. When the specific condition programmed into the virus is met, the virus will launch and infect files in the folder or directory specified in the AUTOEXEC.BAT file path. These viruses are usually found in the hard disk's root directory. Your typical antivirus scanner should detect and eliminate these viruses. They generally have little impact on the computer's performance.

Memory Resident Virus

These guys hang out in the computer memory and are activated when the operating system runs. It then affects any files that are opened. This virus will hide in the RAM and stays there after the code has been executed. It gains control of the system memory and allocates memory blocks for it to run its own code on when any function is performed. It will corrupt programs and files that are opened, closed, renamed, copied, etc. This is another virus that your antivirus software should protect you from.

Polymorphic Virus

A polymorphic virus encodes or encrypts itself in a different way every time it infects a system. It does this by using different encryption keys and algorithms every time. Due to this, it is hard for an average antivirus software to find them using signature or string searches. This is where a more high-end antivirus is useful as they are more likely to catch them.

Macro Virus

These are intended to infect files that are made using certain programs or applications that contain macros, like .xls, .doc, and .pps. These viruses automatically infect files that contain macros and can also infect the documents and templates that the file contains. It is known as a type of e-mail virus. The best way to protect yourself from these viruses is to use common sense when opening e-mails and to avoid opening ones sent from unknown senders. You can also disable macros on your computer for further protection.

Overwrite Virus

Deleting the information contained in the files that it infects is how this virus got its name. This leaves the files either partially or totally useless. The virus will replace the content of the file but not change the file size. In order to get rid of this virus, you must delete the file, and you will lose your original content. They are easy to detect, however, because they render the original program useless.

FAT Virus

FAT stands for file allocation table and it is the part of a disk used for the information on the location of files, unusable space, and available space. These viruses may damage crucial information and it can prevent access to sections of the disk where vital files are stored. This can result in the loss of information from individual files or even entire directories. To avoid these viruses, take basic safety precautions such as running an updated virus scan often. You should also avoid plugging things into your computer, such as a friend's digital camera, as FAT viruses can travel that way as well.

Multipartite Virus

This type of virus spreads in a multitude of ways. How it operates depends on the operating system installed and what files are present. They will hide in the memory initially, like resident viruses, and then move on to infect the hard disk. In order to get rid of this type of virus, you need to clean the boot sector and the disk, and reload all of the data. Ensure that the data you are reloading is clean.

Chapter 5:
Hacker Culture

There is a subculture of individuals who considered themselves part of the "hacker culture." These people enjoy using creativity and persistence to overcome challenges. They earn respect by doing what has not been done before and then sharing their knowledge with the community.

As individuals, hackers may often seem antisocial. Working on a program can be lonely work that involves hours spent in front of a computer. With the invention of the internet, however, hackers could communicate and a subculture was born.

Many hackers do not have malicious intent, but instead view a secure system as a hiker would view Mt. Everest. Hacking into it is a challenge that, if completed, would earn them a massive amount of respect and bragging rights.

One thing almost all hackers can agree on is in their support of open-source software. These are programs in which the code is available for anyone to study, modify, copy, or distribute. This allows hackers to learn from each other's experiences and improve on their findings. Remember, most hackers are after knowledge above all else.

Many members of the hacking community very much wish that people would stop using the term "hacker" to refer to the people that they call "crackers." Crackers are the ones with the malicious intent and have unfortunately given them all a bad name. That being said, many hackers that do not have malicious intent still break the law on a regular basis while pursuing their passion.

There are several ways that hackers stay in touch with each other. There is a hacker journal known as "2600: The Hacker Quarterly" which can be found both online and in print. There is also a website called hacker.org that is full of information as well as puzzles and tests for hackers to try out and compete with. There are also annual hacker events, such as DEFCON in Las Vegas and Chaos Communication Camp. Most hacking events promote safe and ethical hacking behavior. At the Chaos Communication Camp, they combine high technology with low-tech living and most of the participants stay in tents.

Hacker Principles and Ethics

There are a few "rules" for belonging to and being accepted by the hacking community.

- All information should be freely exchanged.

- Hackers should be judged on ability, not things like degrees, age, race, etc.

- An attitude that computers can change anyone's life for the better.

- A belief that you can create beauty and art on a computer.

- Wanting access to computers to be free and total so that everyone may learn more about the world.

A term often used in the community is "hack value." Something that is perceived as difficult to do has a lot of hack value. Doing something in an unconventional way, such as using a computer mouse as a barcode scanner, has a lot of hack value. If within the community a project is said to have hack value, it means that it has been determined to be interesting and worthwhile.

Chapter 6:
Hacking and the Law

Most government and law enforcement officials do not have warm and fuzzy feelings about hackers. This is due to their ability to gain access to classified information, or intelligence, whenever the mood strikes them. If you are ever caught hacking, it is unlikely that the government who catches you will care what your motivation is. They will more than likely treat you like a spy with wicked intentions.

There are several laws in the United States designed to deter people from hacking. Punishments for getting caught hacking range from some rather hefty fines to some serious jail time. Your first minor offense may earn you 6 months of probation, while other more serious offenses can earn you up to 20 years in prison. The penalties are based on the fact that the crimes can be classified anywhere from a class B misdemeanor to a class B felony. One of the deciding factors is how much money is involved in the crime and how many people were affected.

Even though it is older, most hacking crimes are still prosecuted under the Computer Fraud and Abuse Act (CFAA) of 18 U.S.C. § 1030. Other laws and codes used to prosecute hackers are the Wiretap Act (18 U.S.C. § 2511,) Unlawful Access to Stored Communications (18 U.S.C. § 2701,) Identity Theft and Aggravated Identity Theft (18 U.S.C. § 1028A,) Access Device Fraud (18 U.S.C. § 1029,) CAN-SPAM Act (18 U.S.C. § 1037,) Wire Fraud (18 U.S.C. § 1343,) and Communications Interference (18 U.S.C. § 1362.)

In addition to the previously mentioned Federal laws, each state has its own laws regarding computer crime. These are called Computer Crime Statues. Some states have more restrictive laws than the federal ones.

Due to the fact that you can commit crimes in a whole other country from the comfort of your living room, extradition becomes a major factor in prosecuting hackers. The petition to extradite someone can take years, even if the country is being cooperative.

All of this information is very important to keep in mind if you decide you want to dabble in hacking. Despite your intentions, you may find yourself in violation of state or federal laws.

The U.S. Department and Federal Bureau of Investigation routinely have hackers on their Most Wanted List, with millions of dollars of rewards being promised to anyone who can lead to their arrest. Most of the people that make this list are not American but a few occasionally make the list. Many of the most wanted hackers are of Syrian, Iranian, and Russian descent.

Chapter 7:
Simple Hacking Techniques

It is important to note that hacking is illegal and if you get caught hacking a system without permission it can have some serious repercussions. If you are not familiar with some of the terms used, refer to Chapter 9 for definitions and examples.

VPNs

In order to have some anonymity in your hacking attempts, it is a good idea to use a VPN, or Virtual Private Network. It creates an encrypted connection to a less secure network. It will help to hide your IP address in case someone tries to track your activity online. There a several sites you can find VPNs on:

- PureVPN – The perks of this service are they have 500+ servers in 141 countries and do not allow third parties to track your usage. They claim to have the fastest speed.

- VyprVPN – One upside of this is the will allow you to try it for free for three days. They have easy to use apps for every device. It is an unlimited service without data caps or restrictions.

- ZenMate VPN – They provide 128-bit AES encryption and have servers in 20 countries. You can try this service for one month for free, but you will have to provide credit card information.

- ExpressVPN – Also coming with a 30-day free trial, this service uses 256-bit AES encryption. It is considered easy to use and has a great online support team in case you need help.

Password Cracking

There are several tools available out there to help you to brute force a password. The brute force method requires trying every possible password. How long this process takes depends on the possible length of the password, making it a time consuming process, even for computers. Not all of them work with all operating systems and it will be up to you to determine which one best works for you.

- Brutus – Probably the most popular of the online tools for cracking a password, Brutus can be used remotely. It claims to be the fastest tool available. It is a free download, but it is only available for Windows.

- Wfuzz – This is a web-application based tool that should be at least tried by beginners. It can be used for finding hidden resources as well as identifying different types of SQL injections.

- John the Ripper – This is a popular password cracking tool that can work on all of the important operating systems. The program is free. It combines a number of password crackers into one convenient package. It auto-detects hash types and includes a customizable cracker.

- THC Hydra – Another password cracker that claims to be faster than the rest, this one is also available on all of the major operating systems and supports various network protocols. It is flexible and new modules are easy to add.

If you decide to engage in ethical hacking, follow these basic steps and see if you can beat the protections in place to keep you out.

Shutting Down Computers Remotely

On your computer, you have the power to shut down just about any other computer on the planet if you have the proper information.

If the computer is on the same network as yours, like in your home, school, or office. You simply need to know its name. The steps for shutting down a computer on your network are:

1. Type cmd on search bar to open command.

2. Optionally, type "color a" (do not include quotes) and hit enter. This simply gives you "hacker colors," which are green and black.

3. Type "net view" and hit enter to see the computers on your network.

4. Type "shutdown -i" and hit enter to bring up a dialog box.

5. Fill out the options in the box, including the name of the computer you want to shut down, the reason for the shutdown, and if you want to display a warning, and if so for how long.

If you want to shut down a computer that is not on your network, you will need an IP address. Since you are an ethical hacker who is doing this for educational purposes, it is a good idea to practice on your own computer. If you do not know your IP address, simply go to www.whatismyip.com to learn it.

Then, follow the previously mentioned steps, except for the fact that you will be entering the IP address in place of the computer's name.

Practicing CMD Prompts

If you have administrator privileges on your computer, you can practice a number of command prompts to get more adept at hacking. As long as you are using your own computer and not torturing family members with these prompts, it is an ethical way to get the hang of CMD.

After opening command prompt, you can add and delete users on your computer, give them administrator privileges, and add or change their password. Use a test account to try the following out:

1. In command prompt, type "net user test /add" and hit enter. The word "test" can be replaced with whatever you want to name your practice account. It should tell you the command completed successfully. You can then go into your control panel to see if the new user account appears.

2. In command prompt, type "net localgroup administrators test /add" and hit enter. This will give your test user account administrative privileges. It should again tell you the command completed successfully.

3. In command prompt, type "net user *" and hit enter. This will now allow you to add a password to this account. It will ask for the password twice to confirm. It more than likely will not show you the characters you

type, likely for security reasons, but rest assured that it is remembering your password.

4. If you want to change the password for your test account, or any other account for that matter, you can do so without knowing the previous password. Simply type "net user *" and hit enter. It will not ask you for the last password, it will just ask you to type the new one twice.

5. In command prompt, type "net user test /delete" and hit enter to delete your test account. You can also abbreviate "delete" down to just "del." This will get rid of the account you just created to test out command prompts.

There are a few other command prompts you will want to familiarize yourself with. They are:

- Ping Host – This will verify contact with the machine host. When entering this command, it sends ICMP (Internet Control Message Protocol) ping packets to a different computer to see how long it takes to respond, if it responds at all. You can send a ping to an IP address or a host name. Type "ping" space and then the name or IP. You can also type "ping -n 100" then the name to send one hundred ping packets. You can replace the number 100. To find other things you can do with ping, type "ping /h"

- Tracert – This command allows you to track the route a packet follows as it travels from your host computer to a destination host. It also tracks how long each "hop" it takes took it. It can trace up to 30 hops and you can specify how many you want it to look at by typing "tracert -n 23" with the number 23 representing how many hops you want. To see more options with tracert type "tracert /?"

- Ipconfig – This will display information of your host's active network interfaces. You can type "ipconfig /all" to show more details. You can also type "ipconfig /renew" to renew your connection with automatic configuration. There is also "ipconfig /release" to deactivate networking. For more options, type "ipconfig /?"

- Route Print – Displays the routing table and can be used to set-up or delete static routes. Type "route print" to display the list of routes, "route add" to add a route, and "route delete" to delete one. For more options, type "route /?"

- Netstat – This will give you information on the status of the network and the established connections with remote devices. Type "netstat – a" to check all of the connections and listening ports. Type "netstat -n" to display port numbers and addresses in numeric form. Type "netstat -e" to sample the Ethernet statistics. You can combine options, like "netstat -an" and as always, to see more options, type "netstat /?"

How to Think Like a Hacker

Thinking like a hacker can help you understand how hacking happens and also how to protect yourself. Consider the following five things:

1. Identify potential exploits and their domain name. Gather as much information as possible so you can

create a footprint analysis. Think about what security systems may be in place, the potential entry points, and the size of the target. Learn the company's phone numbers, domain names, IP networks, and subsidiaries.

2. Look for a "back door" entry point. A good tip for this is to look for smaller companies that have recently been bought by bigger ones. Startups often have weak security and can give a hacker entry to the network. Hacking the small company may provide insights into the networks and security of the bigger corporation.

3. Connect to the listening TCP and UDP ports of your target and send some random data. This will help to determine the version of File Transfer Protocol, Web, or mail servers they are using. Many TCP and UDP services will identify the running application based on its response to your random data. In order to find exploits, cross reference your findings with a vulnerability scanner such as SecurityFocus.

4. Think about how you will gain access once your reconnaissance is done. You will need a username and password. These are generally acquired through a sneak attack of some kind. This means that hackers will find information on the company's website or perhaps call and talk to an employee while pretending to be tech support. This is obviously risky and one would not want to get caught doing it. Fact is, many unsuspecting employees will give information if the hacker manages to sound authoritative enough.

5. Once you have obtained log-in information, it is time to "Trojan" the system. You can enter the username and

password and insert code to replace something on the system. An example would be replacing notepad.exe with a piece of Trojan code. Ideally, this code would allow the hacker to become an administrator on the system and have access to "admin only" information.

Chapter 8:
How to Protect Yourself

After reading about how easy hacking can be and how widespread it is, you may be wondering how to protect yourself from it. The biggest thing you can do is employ some healthy skepticism when surfing the web and to educate yourself on your operating system and system software. Use the following steps to keep your information out of the hands of hackers:

1. Install Antivirus Software – Have an antivirus program installed (and kept updated.) Look for something with capabilities like "surf web safely" or "protect my identity." Norton and McAfee are both very famous producers of antivirus software. There are free programs available to download as well, such as Malwarebytes and Avast.

2. Secure Your Home Network – Ensure that your home wireless network is password protected. Change the default password that comes with your router- many hackers know these. Having an open network is just asking for trouble. You will also want a firewall in place. Many routers come with one already pre-installed.

3. Think Twice About Email Attachments – Email attachments are a favorite of hackers and they will try to make you think you are opening something from a trusted source. Be careful what you click on, it is unlikely your bank or the government are sending you attachments.

4. Avoid Questionable Sites – You can download something such as Norton Site Web to tell you if the website you are on is secure.

5. Do Not Click on Ads – No matter how tempting, avoid clicking on ads you see online. If you are really interested in a product, try to find its legitimate website.

6. Do Not Fall for Alarming Pop-Ups – You may have had something pop-up while browsing warning you that your computer has been compromised or is experiencing critical errors. Do not click "Okay," "Continue," or whatever it is asking you to do. These are hacking attempts 100% of the time.

7. Stay Off of the Cloud – The Cloud has been a wonderful tool for connecting people and coworkers and sharing information across multiple devices. However, hackers love to attack the Cloud, so avoid putting anything on it you would not want to fall into their hands.

8. Avoid Free Wi-Fi – It is important to stay off free Wi-Fi as much as possible, and when you do have to use it assume that hackers are watching and act accordingly.

9. Stay Off Public Computers – It is not possible for everyone to stay off public computers, but if it is possible for you, do not use them. The more people that use a computer the more likely it is to have gotten a virus.

10. Clear Your Browser History – It is easy for someone to track your internet usage by viewing your browsing history. It is a good idea to clear your history on a daily

basis on all of your devices, including computers, tablets, and smartphones.

11. Update Your Software – Operating system and web browser updates can help close loopholes that hackers have figured out how to exploit. Check for updates often and download them.

12. Use HTTPS – It stands for "hyper-text transfer protocol secure." Sites that support HTTPS connections have an additional layer of encryption, better securing the information exchanged between you and the site. Additionally, the information on the site has been authenticated.

13. Change Your Passwords – Make your passwords difficult to guess and change them frequently. Avoid using one password for every site. In fact, every site should have its own password. That way, if one database is hacked, your password can only be used on the one site. There are password management sites such as 1Password and LastPass to help you keep it all straight.

14. Password Difficulty – In addition to changing your password often, make it hard to hack. Use a variety of upper and lower case letters, numbers, and special characters. Resist the urge to use a pet's name or your child's date of birth.

15. Passcode Your Phone – As much as it may become a nuisance, having a passcode on your phone will protect it from nosey people after your private information.

16. Get Creative with Security Questions – In this day and age, it is not that hard to figure out what high school someone graduated from or even what their mother's maiden name was. Answering questions in a clever way is a good way to protect your information.

17. Turn Off Your Computer – If you are not going to be using your computer for a while, shutting it down is a surefire way to make sure no one is accessing your personal information.

18. Destroy All Traces of Personal Info – If you plan on selling any hardware, be sure to eliminate all traces of yourself on your hard drive. Run something like d-ban to erase most of the personal data. If you are really concerned or have especially sensitive data on your hard drive, simply do not let it into anyone else's hands. A hammer would ensure no one ever got their hands on your information!

19. Watch for Signs of Spyware – Signs that you have been infected include your computer running much slower all of a sudden, a sudden barrage of pop-ups, new toolbars or icons appear on your computer, your homepage has changed, or you are constantly getting random Windows error messages.

20. If in Doubt – If you think there is a chance you have been hacked, immediately change your passwords and keep a close eye on your bank and credit card accounts. The sooner you can catch fraudulent activity, the sooner it can be stopped and the easier it will be to prove you should not be held financially responsible.

Chapter 9:
Terms a Hacker Should Know

Refer to the following glossary while on your journey into hacking and to help in the protection of your own personal information.

- **Back Door** – Also known as a trap door, this is a hidden entry into a computer program that allows a hacker to bypass security features such as requiring a password.

- **Bot** – A program that automatically does a simple action, used for repeating the action over and over. They are usually the tools used in a DoS attack. Bot can also be the term for a hijacked computer on a Botnet.

- **Botnet** – A group of computers being controlled without their owners' knowledge and used for hacking purposes, such as sending out spam or making DoS attacks. Malware can be used to hijack the individual computer, turning them into "zombies" and sending directions through them. This was a popular tactic in the former Soviet Union.

- **Brute Force Attack** – Considered an inefficient method of hacking, this involves an automated search for every possible password for a system.

- **C Programming Language** – An incredibly popular programming language for creating computer programs. It is used for creating system and application software.

- **Code** – A language for machines, it is usually text-based instructions that govern the behavior of a device or a program. Modifying the code modifies the behavior.

- **Cookie** – Text files sent from your web browser to a server. This information is used to customize information presented on the website.

- **Doxing** – Finding out and then publishing other users' anonymous information. This is done by tracing their publicly available accounts as well as by hacking and stalking.

- **Encryption** – An effective way to achieve security, encryption requires you to have a special key or password that allows you to decrypt data. Unencrypted data is called plain text, and encrypted data is called cipher text.

- **Glitch** – A temporary and sudden disruption or irregularity of equipment. It is usually a minor problem that is easy to fix.

- **IP** – Internet protocol address. It is a distinctive numerical fingerprint that identifies a device as it connects to a network using Internet Protocol. They are assigned by the Internet Assigned Numbers Authority (IANA.) With the IP, you can track a device's location, identify the person using it, and track its activity.

- **Kernel** – The computer program that makes up the central core of a computer's operating system. It is also called the nucleus. It controls absolutely everything that happens within the system, from start-up to shut-down.

- **Linux** – Simply put, Linux is an open-source operating system based on UNIX. What makes it different is the Linux Kernel, which was released in 1991.

- **Malware** – A software program that has been designed to hijack, damage, or steal information from a system or a device. It is delivered in a variety of ways, from emails, decoy websites, and USB drives. Some examples are adware, viruses, keyloggers, and root kits.

- **Proxy** – When you make a request on the internet, your computer generally connects directly to the end server. A proxy acts as the middle-man. Your computer sends its request to the proxy, which contacts the end server, and the response is relayed back the same way. It can be used to maintain anonymity as well as to bypass security/parental controls.

- **Root Kit** – This is a software package designed to give an unauthorized user control of a computer system, ideally without being detected.

- **Spyware** – A type of malware that hides on a computer or network and sends back information to the hacker. Useful for collecting usernames, passwords, and financial information.

- **SQL** – Stands for Structured Query Language. It is the main language used to communicate with a database.

- **TCP** – Stands for Transmission Control Protocol. It provides a reliable and error-checked stream of information in the form of octets between devices running on an IP network. The World Wide Web, email servers, file transfers, and remote administration all rely heavily on TCP.

- **Trojan Horse** – A type of malware that pretends to be a desirable piece of software. It delivers its payload and often establishes a back door into the network.

- **UDP** – Stands for User Datagram Protocol. It is one of the core members of the Internet Protocol Suite. It uses a simple connectionless transmission model.

- **UNIX** - A very popular multi-user system. It comes from the AT &T Unix developed in the 1970s. It is the first portable operating system, and is written using the C programming language, allowing it to reach multiple platforms.

- **Zero-Day Attack** - Also known as Zero-Day Exploits, these are attacks on unpatched vulnerabilities that are publicly known.

- **Zombie** – A computer that has been compromised through a computer virus or Trojan horse that is connected to the internet and can be used to perform malicious tasks remotely.

If you want to fit in while browsing the hacker forums, or simply be able to follow the conversation, try adding some of these hacker slang terms to your vocabulary.

Hacker Slang Terms

- **Bit Rot** – This can also be called 'bit decay', and it is used to explain how bits decay as if they were radioactive. Even programs and features that have not been used will eventually have problems even if nothing about them has changed.

- **Copybroke** – Sometimes called 'copywrong', this is used to describe a copyrighted program who has had its protections disabled. It can also refer to copyrighted programs that have been rendered unusable due to a bug or bit-rot that is confusing an anti-piracy check.

- **Crayola** – A super mini or microcomputer that provides a percentage of a supercomputer's power for a fraction of the price.

- **Cruft** – A term used to describe excessive, garbage code. It is commonly used to define superfluous and redundant code. This is one of the oldest slang terms around in the hacking community.

- **Dinosaur** - Hardware that requires raised flooring and special power. Used to refer to older technology and sometimes a very conservative computer user.

- **Easter Egg** – A joke hidden within the code meant to be hunted for, like children hunt for eggs on Easter. Personal computers often have elaborately hidden Easter Eggs that say things like the developers' names, snatches of music, and political messages.

- **Epsilon** – A small quantity, too small to matter generally. Close enough to be indistinguishable for all practical purposes. It can also mean that it is not close enough, but not much will be required to get it there.

- **Finger** – Term used for a program that displays a particular user or even all of the users logged into a particular network or system. Typically shows the username, last time logged in, and the terminal location.

- **Fritterware** – An excessive capability that serves no productive end. Something that eats a huge amount of time for small gains and yet people do it anyway.

- **Hacked Off** – A popular term amongst hackers, this is a play on terms such as "ticked off." Usually used in terms of system administrators who are suspicious that their code has been or is going to be used for criminal activity.

- **Hamster** – A particularly smooth piece of code that is designed to do one thing and does it well. It is a small, well-contained hack that reminds people of a hamster spinning on its wheel. It can also refer to a wireless mouse.

- **Jupiter** – To end an IRC robot or user and then preventing it from reconnecting by adopting its nickname.

- **Larval Stage** – A stage passed through by fledgling hackers, it involves going through a period where the person only focuses on hacking. It can last six months to two years, with the average person staying in it 18 months.

- **Sandbox** – A common term used to describe the research and development stage at many software and computer companies.

- **Spaghetti Code** – Code with a tangled and complex structure, particularly ones using exceptions, GOTOs, and other "unstructured" branching constructs.

Conclusion

Thanks again for taking the time to read this book!

You should now have a good understanding of hacking, and be able to complete some basic hacks.

If you enjoyed this book, please take the time to leave me a review on Amazon. I appreciate your honest feedback, and it really helps me to continue producing high quality books.

CPSIA information can be obtained
at www.ICGtesting.com
Printed in the USA
LVHW021545011119
636085LV00010B/537/P

HACKING

Hacking is a skill that has been refined and developed over the years, and has recently risen to popularity in the computing world.
Yet still, many hackers are grossly misunderstood.

This book explains the different types of hackers, and their motivations for hacking.

It also includes the different types of hacks that can be done, and will teach you how to complete some basic hacks yourself!

If you'd like to learn more about hacking, and begin learning how to hack - then this book is where you need to start!

ISBN 978-1-925989-51

T2-FEI-849

PROTECTION DOGS

For You And Your Family

Edward Weiss, M.D.
Thomas G. Rose

ANOTHER DENLINGER BOOK